FIGHTING FOR A GREENER PLANET

AL GORE

FIGHTING FOR A GREENER PLANET

AL GORE

Rebecca Stefoff

Lerner Publications Company · Minneapolis

For my young friend Calvin Blackheart

The images in this book are used with the permission of: © Jean Baptiste Lacroix/ WireImage/Getty Images, p. 2; AP Photo/John McConnico, p. 6; AP Photo/Joe Rudis/ The Tennessean, p. 9; AP Photo, pp. 10, 14, 15, 20, 22; AP Photo/Harvard Yearbook Publications, p. 13; AP Photo/The Tennessean, Billy Easley, p. 17; © Jeffrey Markowitz/ Sygma/CORBIS, pp. 18, 24, 27; © James Keyser/Time & Life Pictures/Getty Images, p. 28; © Walter Dhladhla/AFP/Getty Images, p. 30; AP Photo/Denis Paquin, p. 32; © Luke Frazza/AFP/Getty Images, p. 34; AP Photo/Ed Reinke, p. 35; AP Photo/Alan Diaz, p. 37; AP Photo/Doug Mills, p. 38; AP Photo/Kevork Djansezian, p. 40.
Front Cover: © Carlos Alvarez/Getty Images (main); NASA/JSC (background).

Text copyright © 2009 by Rebecca Stefoff

Lerner Publications Company
A division of Lerner Publishing Group, Inc.
241 First Avenue North
Minneapolis, MN 55401 U.S.A.

Website address: www.lernerbooks.com

Library of Congress Cataloging-in-Publication Data

Stefoff, Rebecca
    Al Gore : fighting for a greener planet / by Rebecca Stefoff. — Rev. ed.
      p.   cm. — (Gateway biographies)
    Original ed.: Brookfield, Conn. : Millbrook Press, © 1994, with title: Al Gore, vice president.
    Includes index.
    ISBN 978-1-57505-948-8 (lib. bdg. : alk. paper)
    1. Gore, Albert, 1948-–Juvenile literature. 2. Vice-Presidents–United States– Biography–Juvenile literature. 3. Environmentalists–United States–Biography– Juvenile literature. 4. Nobel Prize winners–United States–Biography–Juvenile literature. 5. Legislators–United States–Biography–Juvenile literature. 6. United States. Congress. Senate–Biography–Juvenile literature. 7. Presidential candidates– United States–Biography–Juvenile literature. I. Stefoff, Rebecca, 1951- Al Gore, vice president. II. Title.
E840.8.G65S74 2009
973.929092–dc22 [B]   2007049050

Manufactured in the United States of America
1 2 3 4 5 6 – BP – 14 13 12 11 10 09

The text of this book is printed on paper made with 30 percent recycled post-consumer waste fibers. Using paper with post-consumer waste fibers helps to protect endangered forests, conserve mature trees, keep used paper out of landfills, save energy in the manufacturing process, and reduce greenhouse gas emissions.

CONTENTS

Al Gore holds the citation and medal for the Nobel Peace Prize at the ceremony in December 2007. Gore won the prize, shared with the United Nations Intergovernmental Panel on Climate Change.

One of the world's most respected international awards is the Nobel Peace Prize. Each year the prize goes to someone who has made an important contribution to world peace. The winner of the prize can be a person or an organization from any country in the world. In 2007 two winners shared the Nobel Peace Prize. One winner was a United Nations (UN) committee of scientists. The other winner was an American named Al Gore.

The prize made headlines around the world, but a lot of people had already heard of Al Gore. Before winning the prize, Gore had a career as a politician. He served in the U.S. Congress, first as a representative and then as a senator. After that, he served as vice president of the United States for eight years. In 2000 he almost became president. Gore did not receive the Nobel Peace Prize for his political service, however. He won it for his environmental activism.

For years Al Gore had been talking and writing about the dangers of global warming. He shared the Nobel Peace Prize with the UN's Intergovernmental

Panel on Climate Change (IPCC). The panel was formed to decide whether Earth is warming and, if so, whether human activity is the cause. The prize honored Gore and the IPCC for adding to our knowledge of how human actions are changing the planet's climate and for telling the world what needs to be done about it.

When Gore heard that he had won the Nobel Peace Prize, he said, "I will accept this award on behalf of all the people that have been working so long and so hard to try to get the message out about this planetary emergency." Gore himself had worked long and hard. Through speeches, two books, and an award-winning movie, he had been telling people about the threat of global warming for a long time.

A passion for the environment has been one of the driving forces in Al Gore's life. It played a big part in his political career. Gore's life in politics was also shaped by his family background. He had been born into a family that worked in government service.

CHILDHOOD AND SCHOOL

Al Gore was born on March 31, 1948. His full name was Albert Arnold Gore Jr. But he was always called Al. His father was called Albert Sr. Al's parents both came from small towns in Tennessee. But Al was born in Washington, D.C., because his father's office was there. Albert Sr. was a U.S. congressman for many years. Al learned a lot

Al Gore Jr. and his family are shown in Nashville, Tennessee, in 1952. *(Left to right)* Nancy, Pauline, Al, and Albert Sr. traveled back and forth between Tennessee and Washington, D.C.

about politics and government from his father.

Al was the second child in his family. His sister, Nancy, was ten years old when he was born. The *Tennessean* is a newspaper from the Gore family's home state. It reported that when Al was born, Nancy called "everybody in the phone directory" to tell them the news. In spite of the difference in their ages, Al and Nancy were good friends from the start.

As a boy, Al had two homes. For part of each year, the Gores lived in a hotel in Washington. The rest of the time, they lived on a family farm near Carthage, Tennessee. Al liked the country better than the city. Years later he remembered that his time on the farm with horses, cows, canoes, and a big river was more fun than being in his family's suite on the eighth floor of the hotel.

Al gets a good-night kiss from his mother, Pauline, before she and Albert Sr. go to a formal White House reception in Washington, D.C., in March 1957.

Young Al had many good times on the farm. He explored the river in his canoe. On hot days, he went swimming. He learned to ride a pony. Life on the farm was not all play, however. Al learned that farming was hard work. He hoed the tobacco patch. He harvested the corn crop. And he looked after the livestock.

The farm also taught Al lessons about caring for the land. He saw that rain flowing in little gullies could wash away the soil. That soil made the land good for farming. With each rainfall, the gullies got bigger. More precious soil was lost. To stop this erosion, the farmers filled in the gullies with stones. Al remembered this lesson later, when he started thinking about how people were changing the environment. He often used the story of the gullies and the stones to show that people can take action to solve problems. And they can do this before the problems get out of control.

Al started school in Carthage. When he got a little older, he went to Saint Albans School, a boys' school in Washington. As a teenager, he liked to come back to the farm to visit his Tennessee friends. They liked to fish, swim, and water-ski. But there was a lot to do in Washington too. Al's parents made sure that he went to museums, art galleries, concerts, and plays. They wanted him to enjoy one of the world's great cities as well as country life.

School kept Al busy. He studied hard and got good grades, all through high school. He studied the required subjects of math, history, and English. But he also got to choose some courses for himself. He chose classes in painting and writing.

Al played football and basketball for Saint Albans. In his senior year, he was captain of the football team. He also served in the student government. He graduated in 1965. Under his Saint Albans yearbook picture, the caption read, "It probably won't be long before Al reaches the top."

From School to War

Something special happened to Al Gore when he graduated from high school. At a graduation party, he met a lively young woman with blond hair. She lived in Arlington, Virginia, close to Washington. Her name was Mary Elizabeth Aitcheson. But everyone called her Tipper.

Al liked Tipper so much that he called her the very next day to ask for a date. Tipper was impressed with the tall, dark-haired boy. He was smart and interesting as well as good-looking. She agreed to go out with him. Soon they were spending a lot of time together.

In fall 1965, Gore started college. He had been accepted at Harvard University, one of the best schools in the United States. Harvard is near the city of Boston, Massachusetts. Tipper graduated from high school a year later. She chose a college in Boston so she could be close to Gore.

Gore worked hard during his four years at Harvard. Government was his main field of study. He spent one

Gore is shown here in his 1969 Harvard yearbook photograph.

summer taking classes in Mexico City, Mexico. He learned to speak Spanish there. He spent another summer working for the *New York Times*. Gore wanted to learn about newspapers because he was interested in writing. He thought about becoming a reporter.

Gore's college years were a time of great change and confusion in the United States. The country was fighting the Vietnam War (1957–1975) in Southeast Asia. But many Americans, especially young people, felt that the war was wrong. They did not think that U.S. troops should be sent to Vietnam. Students at many colleges protested against the war. They took control of buildings or stayed away from classes. Some young men broke the law by refusing to sign up for the draft, the system by which they could be drawn into the armed forces.

Gore believed the Vietnam War was wrong. But he felt torn. He did not support the war, but he had too much respect for the law to break it. His father also disapproved of the war. But Al Sr. was struggling to win an election to stay in the Senate. If Gore tried to avoid the draft, he could hurt his father's chance to be reelected.

Gore wrestled with this problem. He knew that other young men, including friends he had grown up with, were facing enemy bullets in Vietnam. How would he feel if he refused to serve his country in a time of war?

Finally, Gore's sense of duty outweighed his feelings against the war. In the summer of 1969, he joined the army. He was sent to an army base in Alabama. There, he was given a job on the base newspaper. The following spring, Gore and Tipper were married in Washington, D.C. They set up their first home in a trailer in Alabama. Six months later, Gore was ordered to Vietnam.

Tipper and Al Gore *(left)* greet Gore's parents after their wedding at Washington Cathedral in 1970.

THE EFFECTS OF WAR

The war had a deep effect on Gore, as it did on most of the Americans who went to Vietnam. Gore served in Vietnam for only six months, and he did not fight in any battles. Instead, he was a combat journalist. His job was to write about the war for army newspapers. Gore saw enough action to make him believe that violence is not how human beings should settle their differences. He wrote to friends that he was haunted by the horrible things he had seen.

Gore in his military uniform during his six months in Vietnam

ENTERING POLITICS

Gore returned to the United States in 1971. His father had retired from the Senate in January that year. Gore and Tipper settled down in Carthage, Tennessee. He started a company to build and sell houses. But real estate did not hold his interest. He began thinking about what he wanted to do with the rest of his life.

Religion had always been important to Gore. As a child, he had gone to Baptist church services with his parents. In 1971 he enrolled in divinity school at Vanderbilt University in Nashville, Tennessee. Divinity school prepares people to be ministers. Gore, however, was not set on becoming a minister. He just wanted a chance to think deeply about life and death, good and evil. Divinity school did not give Gore all the answers he looked for. But he said that it taught him to ask "better questions."

Meanwhile, Gore returned to writing. He took a job as a reporter on the *Tennessean*. Tipper went to work for the *Tennessean* too, as a photographer. Soon the Gores moved to Nashville to be closer to the newspaper offices. Their first child, a daughter named Karenna, was born there in 1973. Three more children followed—Kristin in 1977, Sarah in 1979, and Albert III in 1982.

Gore was a newspaper writer. And he enjoyed the job. His favorite stories were those in which he exposed shady deals or bad government. As time went on, Gore wanted to do more than write about such problems. He wanted to help solve them. In 1975 he started law

Gore *(right)* worked as a reporter at the Nashville *Tennessean*. Here he works with chief photographer, Bill Preston, in 1974.

school at Vanderbilt University. By the next year, however, Gore felt he was ready to move on to public service full-time.

In 1976 Gore ran for Congress. He ran for the same seat that his father had first won thirty-eight years earlier. If the people of Tennessee voted him into office, Gore would become a member of the U.S. House of Representatives.

He made his first campaign speech on the courthouse steps in Carthage. A crowd gathered on the street to hear him. After his speech, he walked down the street. He shook hands with everyone he met and

Gore *(left)* shakes hands with a voter while on the campaign trail in July 1976. Gore ran for his father's old seat in the U.S. Congress.

asked them to vote for him. He felt very awkward at first. But after he had shaken hands with ten or twelve people, his confidence grew. He started to feel more comfortable.

Gore won the support of the Democratic Party. On Election Day, he saw that the voters believed in him too. He won the election. And he was reelected to the same seat three times. Gore served a total of eight years in the House of Representatives.

During those years, Gore built a reputation for hard work and honesty. Unlike some representatives, he rarely missed a vote or other important House business. He also found time to return to his district almost every weekend. He met with people to listen to their concerns. During his eight years in the House, he held sixteen hundred of these meetings—more than any other representative before him.

Many of Gore's projects in the House of Representatives dealt with health. He helped pass laws that forced cigarette and liquor companies to put stronger warning labels on their products. The labels warned of the dangers of tobacco and alcohol. He worked on plans to help the homeless and people with AIDS. He also worked to pass laws that made it illegal for companies to sell baby food that did not meet health standards.

CONCERN FOR THE ENVIRONMENT

In 1978 a Tennessee family wrote to their congressman, Al Gore. The family told Gore that chemicals dumped near their farm had made them sick. Gore investigated the matter and discovered that several million gallons of hazardous waste had been dumped into ditches in that part of Tennessee. The waste was leaking into people's wells and poisoning their water.

Gore set up meetings in Congress to make the other representatives aware of the problems of dumping toxic waste. These were the first meetings that the government had ever held on the subject. As a result, two years later Congress passed a law creating the Superfund. Government money was set aside to clean up the worst toxic waste dumps. Gore was one of the authors of that law.

Interest in the environment was not new to Congressman Gore. He had been thinking about environmental problems since long before he entered politics.

As a teenager, Gore had read *Silent Spring*, by Rachel Carson. In that book, Carson talked about the chemicals that farmers used in the 1950s and 1960s

Rachel Carson testifies before Congress in 1963. Carson warned about the use of chemicals in the 1950s and 1960s. Carson's book *Silent Spring* had a profound effect on Gore.

to protect their crops from insects. She warned that these poisons were killing many kinds of animals, birds, and fish.

When Gore went to Harvard, one of his teachers was Roger Revelle. He was one of the first scientists to measure the increase in carbon dioxide, a gas that is part of the air. Scientists call carbon dioxide a greenhouse gas. That means that carbon dioxide keeps the sun's heat from bouncing off Earth. Greenhouse gases, like glass windows in a greehouse, reflect the heat back down onto Earth's surface.

Revelle found that the amount of carbon dioxide in the air was rising. He believed that the increase came from people's use of fossil fuels. These fuels are coal, oil, and gasoline. They are made from the fossilized remains of ancient plants and animals.

When fossil fuels burn, they release carbon dioxide into the air. Revelle and some other scientists began to think that if the amount of carbon dioxide kept increasing, a "greenhouse effect" would warm Earth. This greenhouse effect would change the planet's climate. Through Revelle, Gore was introduced to these ideas while he was in college.

A few years later, during Gore's time in Vietnam, he saw U.S. soldiers use powerful chemicals to kill trees so the enemy could not hide in the forests. Gore remembered Rachel Carson's warnings in *Silent Spring*. He wondered, Do we really know what we are doing when we spray these poisons into our air?

Roger Revelle was a professor of Gore's at Harvard and an environmental expert. He appeared before Congress to talk about global warming concerns.

Gore carried his concerns about the environment to his job as a congressman. In addition to holding government meetings about toxic waste, he invited Roger Revelle to talk to Congress about global warming.

Global warming became the subject of angry debates in Congress and in the media. Oil and coal companies dismissed global warming as nonsense. Carmakers were upset that global warming was being blamed on greenhouse gases in the exhaust from millions and millions of automobiles. Some scientists claimed that global warming had not been fully proved.

Over time, however, many of the world's leading scientists came to agree that global warming is real and that the world is warming up. Water flows into the oceans from melting glaciers and polar ice formations. The additional water makes the sea level rise. Cities and towns on low-lying seacoasts are at risk of flooding. Global warming is changing the climate enough to turn some fertile farmlands into desert and to warm the regions near the North Pole and the South Pole.

Big questions about global warming concern the role of human activities, such as burning fossil fuels. Scientists know that Earth's climate has changed many times over millions of years—although usually not as fast as it is changing in modern times. How much climate change is caused by people? Should people change their way of life to create fewer greenhouse gases? If people do make changes, will the changes be enough to make a difference in global warming?

While some people argued over those questions, Al Gore started speaking out about the dangers of global warming. He felt that the evidence for climate change was strong. Gore urged lawmakers and ordinary people to cut down on the greenhouse gases we are adding to the air, so that we can limit climate change as much as possible. To make his point about global warming, Gore often used the old saying, "when you're in a hole, stop digging."

NUCLEAR ARMS

In 1980 Gore made a speech at a girls' school in Tennessee. He was shocked when nearly all the girls said that they thought a nuclear war would happen in their lifetimes. This made him sad and angry. What a horrible way to grow up, expecting worldwide destruction at any moment, Gore thought.

Gore began to study the nuclear arms race. This "race" was a deadly competition between the United

States and the Union of Soviet Socialist Republics (USSR), the other world superpower at the time. (The USSR included Russia and fourteen other countries in eastern Europe and northern Asia.) Each side had built and stored enough nuclear weapons to destroy the other side if a war broke out.

Before long, Gore was an expert on the issue of nuclear arms. Even people in the Republican Party, the Democrats' rival party, said that Gore was one of the top nuclear experts in Congress. Gore encouraged Republican president Ronald Reagan to be more flexible about making deals with the USSR. He encouraged the president to get both countries to destroy some of their nuclear bombs. Gore was proud to think that during his time as a member of the U.S. Congress, he had helped make the world a safer place.

The Gore family is shown here in 1984. *(Left to right, back row)* Albert III, Al, Karenna, and Tipper; *(front row)* Kristin and Sarah.

In the Senate

In 1984 Al Gore felt ready to move from the House of Representatives to the U.S. Senate. He campaigned for one of the two Senate seats from Tennessee.

In the middle of his campaign, Gore received tragic news. His beloved sister, Nancy, who had been a heavy smoker, was dying of lung cancer. Gore spent hours at Nancy's side during her last days. He was deeply shaken by her death. But he managed to carry on with his campaign. On Election Day, Gore won more votes than any other candidate in Tennessee history. He took office as a senator in January 1985.

In the Senate, Gore continued to work on health care, nuclear arms control, and the environment. After a few years, though, he began to think about the next step in his political career. He believed that the United States needed a big change in leadership. He also knew that he had good ideas to offer. After long talks with his family, Gore decided to run for president in 1988.

Other hopeful Democrats had the same idea. More than half a dozen of them competed in state primary elections. The Democrats did not choose Gore as their presidential candidate that year. Instead, they chose Michael Dukakis, the governor of Massachusetts. Gore returned to his duties as a senator. When voters went to the polls, they elected a Republican president, George H. W. Bush.

Tragedy again struck the Gore family in the spring of 1989. Gore took his six-year-old son, Albert, to a baseball game in Baltimore, Maryland, not far from Washington. After the game, they left the stadium and walked across the parking lot. Young Albert slipped away from his father's hand and ran into the path of a car. He was hit and seriously injured.

In the dark days and nights after the accident, Al and Tipper Gore did not know whether Albert would ever get well. Fortunately, Albert recovered from the accident, but he had to have several operations, and he spent a long time in the hospital.

Gore spent hours at the boy's bedside. Sometimes, while Albert slept, Gore thought about what he had achieved during his life. He also thought about what he still hoped to accomplish. He thought about his four children and all the other children in the world. What kind of future would they have? Would Earth be a safe, comfortable home for them when they grew up?

In his son's hospital room, Gore began writing a book about the environmental issues he had studied. He wrote about a trip he had made years before to the South Pole. There, he had watched scientists measure the damage that people had done to Earth's atmosphere. He wrote about a visit to the Amazon River in Brazil. The sky there was black with smoke from the burning rain forest. Gore also told of a slaughtered elephant he had seen in Africa. Its ivory tusks had been sawed out of its head by illegal hunters.

Gore's trip to the South Pole shaped his thoughts on the environment. While he was there, scientists were measuring the pollution in Earth's atmosphere.

Gore called his book *Earth in the Balance*. He hoped it would make people think about protecting the planet and its fragile riches instead of using them up or destroying them. "We must all become partners in a bold effort to change the very foundation of our civilization," he wrote.

Earth in the Balance was published in 1992. Many people, including some scientists, disagreed with Gore's information and ideas. Still, the book became a best seller and won Gore the support of people in the environmental movement.

A Hardworking Vice President

In 1992 the Democratic Party chose Bill Clinton, the governor of Arkansas, as its candidate for president. Gore thought Clinton would make a good president. Clinton liked and admired Gore. He knew that Gore was an expert

The Gore and Clinton families take the stage at the Democratic National Convention in New York City, in July 1992. *(Left to right)* Kristin, Sarah, Karenna, Albert III, Gore, Tipper, Bill Clinton, Hillary Rodham Clinton, and Chelsea Clinton.

on the environment and nuclear arms, among other things. Clinton asked Gore to be his running mate, and Gore agreed. Four years after he failed to become a candidate for president, Gore was running for vice president.

He and Clinton made an impressive team. The two young men, both from the South, took on the Republican Party and President George H. W. Bush. Clinton debated the president. Gore debated the vice president, Dan Quayle. Crisscrossing the country in buses, Clinton and Gore promised to make changes in the way government worked.

Clinton said that he would heal the ailing economy

of the United States and create jobs for the growing number of jobless workers. Many Americans liked this message. Environmental groups, too, supported the Democrats because Gore was part of the team.

And the voters responded. In November 1992, Bill Clinton and Al Gore won a strong victory. In January 1993, they were sworn into office as president and vice president of the United States.

The vice president's job has always been difficult to define. Some vice presidents have been very active. Others have done almost nothing. President Clinton made it clear from the start that Gore would have important responsibilities as vice president.

One of Gore's jobs was serving as the head of the Senate, a task that every vice president has performed. Gore had plenty of other duties as well. Clinton put him in charge of all the government programs and committees that dealt with the environment, energy, and new technology.

The president also gave Gore a challenging new assignment called reinventing government. He told Gore to spend six months surveying the entire U.S. government. He was to look for ways to make the government work better and spend less money. Soon, Gore had earned a reputation as one of the hardest-working vice presidents in American history.

Every week President Clinton shared a private lunch with Gore. The lunch provided a time when they could talk about issues in the news and about the country's future. Gore also went to many of the president's meetings. Clinton respected Gore's knowledge of complicated subjects and his ability to make tough decisions.

One of Gore's main jobs was building and maintaining strong relationships with other countries. He went to South Africa for the swearing-in ceremony of Nelson Mandela, that nation's first black president. Gore held meetings with Russian leaders. After those meetings, the United States and Russia began working together on energy, technology, and space programs. Later, Gore visited China to discuss relations between the two countries.

South African President Nelson Mandela *(left)* shakes hands with Vice President Gore in 1995.

Closer to home, Gore's reinventing government project had some success. Gore cut costs in many government departments. Republicans in Congress, however, pointed out that Gore's reforms didn't save as much money as he had claimed they would.

In 1996 Bill Clinton and Al Gore campaigned for reelection. They ran against Bob Dole and Jack Kemp, the Republican candidates for president and vice president. One of the strongest moments in the Democrats' campaign came when Gore debated Kemp on issues such as foreign affairs and the economy. Most viewers agreed that Gore won the debate. A few months later, the Democrats won the election. Clinton and Gore began four more years as the country's top leaders.

Both men faced difficulties during their second term. Questions about Clinton's personal life led to an impeachment (being charged with a serious crime by the House of Representatives). The Senate found Clinton not guilty, but his misbehavior and the impeachment were huge embarrassments for the Democratic Party.

Gore was accused of a different kind of wrongdoing in connection with raising money to pay for the 1996 campaign. It seemed that he had made telephone calls from his White House office asking for contributions. That is against the law. Gore faced hard questions about the phone calls and other fund-raising activities. In the end, though, he was not charged with anything illegal. And through it all, he continued to do his job.

The Internet became another source of trouble for Al Gore. During the eight years of the Clinton-Gore administration, the Internet came into wide use in schools, businesses, and people's homes. Gore looked forward to the day when all American schools, homes, and libraries would be able to connect to the information superhighway of the Internet.

Gore *(left)* and President Clinton watch two California students surf the Internet in 1996.

In Congress and as vice president, Gore helped shape several laws that made it easier for the Internet to operate. Then, in 1999, he gave a television interview in which he said, "During my service in the United States Congress I took the initiative in creating the Internet."

Gore meant that he had led Congress toward making the laws that helped the Internet develop and grow. People who didn't like Gore and his ideas, however, twisted his words. They said that he had claimed to be the inventor of the Internet. This became a way for people to make fun of Gore. But many scientific and business leaders pointed out that Gore really had been an important early supporter of the Internet. He had contributed to its development.

The world environment also continued to concern Gore. Some of the environmentalists who had voted for him were disappointed. They felt he did not do as much to protect forests, air quality, and endangered species as they had hoped. Yet carmakers and other business leaders criticized Gore as a "green" politician. They said that he put the environment ahead of jobs and the economy. Gore learned that balancing the needs and desires of different groups was a challenge.

Gore's years in Congress and as vice president gave him broad experience in government. In 2000, with his time as vice president drawing to an end, he used that experience in one of the greatest challenges of his life—a presidential campaign.

RUNNING FOR PRESIDENT

Back in 1988, Gore had tried to become the Democratic Party's candidate for president. He had failed then, but in 2000, after two terms as vice president, he was the party's choice to run for president. Gore chose Joseph Lieberman, a senator from Connecticut, as his vice-presidential candidate.

During the campaign, Gore and Tipper, with their oldest daughter, Karenna, traveled back and forth across the country making speeches to voters. Gore was running against two main challengers for president. The Republican candidate was George W. Bush, the governor of Texas and son of former president George H. W. Bush. A consumer rights activist named Ralph Nader was the candidate of a much smaller political group called the Green Party.

Gore picked Connecticut senator Joseph Lieberman *(left)* as his running mate in the 2000 presidential campaign.

George W. Bush *(left)* speaks as Gore watches during one of their debates during the 2000 race for president.

The economy of the United States had done very well during President Clinton's eight years in office. This made many Democrats hope that the nation's voters would elect a Democrat for president again. But other Democrats worried that Nader might draw votes away from Gore. Nader, after all, had the support of some environmentalists. No one, however, could have predicted what happened when Americans went to the polls on November 7, 2000.

The election was one of the closest in U.S. history—so close that the television news broadcasters, in their hurry to be the first to announce the winner, kept making mistakes. At one point, it seemed that Bush was going to win. Gore called him on the telephone to concede, or give up, the contest.

But a short time later, more votes were counted. It looked as though Gore might have a chance after all. He called Bush back to "un-concede." Gore was not willing to give up until he was sure that he could not possibly win. One of Gore's biggest disappointments during that long night was that he lost Tennessee. Gore's home state favored Bush.

Across the nation, more Americans voted for Gore than for Bush. Gore won 50,999,897 popular votes, as the votes cast by citizens are called. Bush won 50,456,002. But the president is not elected by the votes of the citizens. Instead, the popular vote within each state says how that state must cast its electoral votes. These electoral votes, known as the electoral college, determine who will be president.

In the election of 2000, the turning point was the state of Florida, where candidate Bush's brother Jeb Bush was governor. Both Al Gore and George Bush needed Florida's electoral votes to win the overall presidential election. When Florida's popular votes were counted, Bush won by 537 votes. This win gave him all of Florida's electoral votes. But the result was so close that Gore asked for the state's popular votes to be recounted.

The recount lasted five weeks. Both sides challenged legal procedures and court decisions. Questions were raised about the accuracy of voting machines and counting methods in Florida and elsewhere.

Many people called
for election reforms
to make sure that
future presidential
contests were fair.

As the days and
weeks of the recount
dragged on, some said
that Gore should give
up the fight. Repub-
licans were angry that
Gore did not con-
cede the election to
Bush. Kristin Gore, Al
and Tipper's middle
daughter, later remembered that some Republicans gathered outside the vice-presidential home in Washington.
She and her family had lived there for the past eight
years. But the Republican gathering screamed at the
Gores to get out.

Gore believed that the Americans who had voted
for him deserved someone who would do everything
possible to make their votes count. Finally, though, the

U.S. Supreme Court stopped the recount. The high court gave Florida's electoral votes to Bush. Al Gore admitted the painful truth. The election was over. He had lost.

On December 13, 2000, Gore made a television appearance to concede the election. "This is America —and we put country before party," he said. "The strength of our American democracy is shown most clearly through the difficulties it can overcome."

Many listeners felt that those words also described Gore. His strength had allowed him to overcome difficulties and disappointments. It had kept him working for what he believed was right. The new question was, What would Al Gore do next?

New Roles

Ever since his days as a junior congressman, Gore had had a reputation as a hard worker. It came as no surprise that he remained busy even when his duties as vice president ended. He turned from politics to life as a private citizen.

Education was one focus of Gore's energy and activity. In 2001 he taught as a visiting lecturer at four different U.S. colleges and universities. They included the journalism schools of Columbia University in New York City and of Middle Tennessee State University. Since then he has continued to visit schools and campuses around the country. He talks to students about government and the environment.

Gore delivered many speeches about global warming. In 2006 he turned his speech on the subject into a documentary movie called *An Inconvenient Truth*. The film was based on the work of hundreds of scientists, as well as on Gore's years of gathering information and studying environmental damage. The same material was published in book form. He titled it *An Inconvenient Truth: The Planetary Emergency of Global Warming and What We Can Do About It*.

The movie and book stirred debate about global warming. A few scientists and some members of the energy industry criticized Gore's facts. They also challenged his claims about the ways climate change will affect human societies. Many others, however, praised

Gore *(left)* and director Davis Guggenheim pose with the Oscar for Best Documentary Feature for 2006. They won for the film *An Inconvenient Truth.*

Gore for calling the world's attention to the problem. The movie version of *An Inconvenient Truth* won an Oscar, or Academy Award, for best documentary of the year.

When Al Gore and the IPCC won the Nobel Peace Prize in the fall of 2007, a few newspaper columnists asked, What does global warming have to do with world peace? Yet Gore has talked many times about the connection between environmental protection and peace.

As climate change turns farmland to desert or causes rivers to dry up, food and water will become scarce in some places. At the same time, if global warming makes the ocean levels rise— as many scientists think they will— millions of people who live near seacoasts will be forced out of their homes. These climate refugees, along with shortages of food and water, will place great strain on the nations of the world, possibly leading to violence.

Gore believes we can bring about a more peaceful world in the future by doing what we can to halt climate change while we have a chance. He has helped start an organization called the Alliance for Climate Protection. The alliance helps people around the world learn what they can do to protect the environment and slow global warming.

Al Gore has been away from political life since leaving the office of vice president in early 2001. His supporters urged him to run for president in 2004, but he did not run. He chose to concentrate on his environmental work.

After the worldwide publicity of the Nobel Peace Prize in 2007, many people who admire Gore hoped that he would enter the race for U.S. president in 2008. Gore would not say for certain that he will not try again to become president. In the weeks after receiving the prize, however, he said many times that he had no plans to run.

Al Gore is one of the world's most respected spokespeople for the environment. By doing what he can to save the planet and by encouraging everyone else to join in protecting the environment, Gore remains a public servant. He is working in the best interests of the whole world.

IMPORTANT DATES

1948	Albert (Al) Gore Jr. is born on March 31 in Washington, D.C.
1969	He graduates from Harvard University and joins the army.
1970	On May 19, he marries Tipper Aitcheson.
1971	In January, Gore goes to Vietnam as a combat reporter.
1976	On November 2, he is elected to the U.S. House of Representatives.
1984	On November 6, he is elected to the U.S. Senate.
1992	He publishes *Earth in the Balance* and becomes Bill Clinton's vice-presidential running mate. Clinton and Gore are elected on November 3.
1996	Clinton and Gore are reelected on November 5.

2000	Gore runs as the Democratic Party's candidate for president. On November 7, he wins the popular vote but loses the electoral vote to Republican George W. Bush.
2006	*An Inconvenient Truth* appears as a film and is published as a book, *An Inconvenient Truth: The Planetary Emergency of Global Warming and What We Can Do About It.*
2007	The documentary movie *An Inconvenient Truth* wins an Academy Award. Gore wins the Nobel Peace Prize.
2008	Gore becomes chairperson of the Emmy Award-winning TV channel Current TV. He is chairperson of Generation Investment Management, a director on the board of Apple Inc., chairperson of the Alliance for Climate Protection, and a partner in the firm Klein Perkins Caufield and Byers, heading its climate change solutions group.
	Two new children's books by Gore—*Know Climate Change* and *101 Q and A on Climate Change*—are released on March 18.
	Gore's new book, *The Path to Survival*, is released on April 22.

GLOSSARY

electoral college: representatives of each state who cast the state's electoral votes. They are chosen to elect the president and vice president, based on how voters in each state vote. States have as many electoral votes as they have members of Congress.

erosion: loss of soil due to the action of wind or water

global warming: the gradual increase in Earth's temperatures, which scientists widely agree occurs due to pollution in the atmosphere, largely because of an increase in greenhouse gases

greenhouse gases: carbon dioxide build up in the atmosphere that works like glass in a greenhouse to trap warmth

hazardous waste: discarded material that contains dangerous substances such as toxic chemicals

popular vote: the total vote cast by the people of the United States on Election Day

Union of Soviet Socialist Republics (USSR): a government that included Russia and fourteen other countries in eastern Europe and northern Asia. It existed between 1922 and 1991.

SOURCE NOTES

8 Walter Gibbs and Sarah Lyall, "Gore Shares Peace Prize for Climate Change Work," *New York Times*, October 13, 2007.

9 Bob Zelnick, *Gore: A Political Life* (Washington, DC: Regnery Publishing, 1999), 27.

16 Peter Steinfels, "Beliefs: In a Wide-Ranging Talk, Al Gore Reveals the Evangelical and Intellectual Roots of His Faith," *New York Times*, May 29, 1999.

27 Al Gore, *Earth in the Balance* (Boston: Houghton Mifflin, 1992), 14.

33 Al Gore, interview by Wolf Blitzer, "Transcript: Vice President Gore on CNN's *Late Edition*," March 9, 1999, http://www.cnn.com/ALLPOLITICS/stories/1999/03/09/president2000/transcript.gore/ (February 21, 2008).

38 Thomas L. Friedman, "Foreign Affairs: Medal of Honor," *New York Times*, December 15, 2000, http://query.nytimes.com/gst/fullpage.html?res=9D0DEFD71F3FF936A25751C1A9669C8B63s cp=18sq=foreign+affairs%3A+medal+of+honortst=nyt (February 22, 2008).

SELECTED BIBLIOGRAPHY

Gore, Al. *The Assault on Reason*. New York: Penguin, 2007.

——. *An Inconvenient Truth: The Planetary Emergency of Global Warming and What We Can Do About It*. Emmaus, PA: Rodale Books, 2007.

Hillin, Hank. *Al Gore: His Life and Career*. Secaucus, NJ: Carol Publishing, 1992.

Maranis, David, and Ellen Nakashima. *The Prince of Tennessee: The Rise of Al Gore*. New York: Simon & Schuster, 2000.

Zelnick, Bob. *Gore: A Political Life*. Washington, DC: Regnery Publishing, 1999.

FURTHER READING AND WEBSITES

Al Gore
http://www.algore.com
Al Gore's website contains information about his life, projects, journal, books, and DVDs.

Benson, Michael. *Bill Clinton.* Minneapolis: Twenty-First Century Books, 2004.

Gore, Al. *An Inconvenient Truth: The Crisis of Global Warming.* Adapted for young readers by Jane O'Connor. New York: Viking, 2007.

Gore, Tipper. *Picture This: A Visual Diary.* New York: Broadway Books, 1996.

Jeffrey, Laura S. *Al Gore: Leader for a New Millennium.* Springfield, NJ: Enslow, 1999.

The Life of Al Gore
http://www.washingtonpost.com/wp-dyn/politics/news/post-series/goreprofiles
This website presents a collection of fifteen *Washington Post* articles on the life of Al Gore, a photo gallery, and a link to related stories.

McCollum, Sean. *Bill Clinton: America's 42nd President.* New York: Children's Press, 2005.

McPherson, Stephanie Sammartino. *Bill Clinton.* Minneapolis: Lerner Publications Company, 2008.

Sapet, Kerrily. *Al Gore.* Greensboro, NC: Morgan Reynolds, 2007.

INDEX